MATH IN THE REAL WORLD OF BUSINESS AND LIVING

Probability, Statistics, and Graphing

by Shirley Cook

Incentive Publications, Inc.
Nashville, Tennessee

Illustrated by Kathleen Bullock
Cover by Geoffrey Brittingham
Edited by Anna Quinn

ISBN 0-86530-343-6

PRINTED IN THE UNITED STATES OF AMERICA

Table of Contents

Preface

Long before the National Council for Teaching Mathematics standards were released, teachers knew the importance of making learning meaningful to students. The standards reinforced the idea that teachers need to help students become problem solvers by linking math to the real world and to other areas of the curriculum. For students, numbers should be more than mere figures on the page—they should represent solutions to real-life situations and problems.

Math in the Real World of Business and Living focuses on real-world links while helping students to refine problem-solving skills. The activities help students realize that numbers-based data and statistics can help them make decisions from what foods they should eat to where they should go to college. Used correctly, numbers can impact their futures in a tremendously positive way.

Students will become involved with studies of surveys and sample populations, probability, statistics, graphing, data analysis, and real-world math application. Each section stands alone for mini lessons or flexible grouping instructions. Students may work independently or in teams or pairs throughout the course of the unit. It will be particularly helpful for students to work together in the Probability and Statistics sections. Students will also need time to complete their classroom surveys.

The Graphing section enhances students' graphing skills while the Real-World Applications section shows them how the information in the graphs is relevant to their lives. In the Data Analysis section, students learn how to interpret charts and graphs and use their new knowledge constructively. The reproducible graphs in the back of the book allow students to create neat, accurate graphs inside or outside of class with minimum inconvenience to teacher and student.

By teaching students how to understand statistics, we can open a whole new world to them. This book was written to show students how statistics, probability, and graphing are applicable to their own lives, how they can use data to make better decisions, and how they can avoid falling into the trap of accepting without question what the statistics tell them.

An Introduction to Probability

How much snow will we get this winter?

Will you win at your computer game?

What will you have for lunch on Saturday?

How many students will be sick on Monday?

Answering questions such as these is not simply a matter of chance. Mathematically, these answers can be assigned some probability of occurrence. Probability is the likelihood that something will happen, estimated as a ratio or a percentage. It is essential in making good business decisions, in research, in forecasting the weather, and in projecting sporting results.

By learning to understand probability, we can make predictions, make informed decisions, and improve our chances of living happy, fulfilled lives. For example, numbers from medical research show us which foods are likely to be carcinogenic, which foods will increase our cholesterol levels, and which foods will help us lose weight. If we use this information to determine our diets, we can reduce our chances of cancer, heart disease, high blood pressure, and obesity as we increase our chances of living longer, healthier lives.

In order to use numbers to make decisions, we must first understand them. This book was written to make probability, statistics, and graphing readily accessible so that they can be applied to everyday life.

Terms

1. Statistics—number facts collected and used to convey information about a particular subject

2. Sample Group—a representative part of the larger whole

3. Random—without any defined method

4. Range—the difference between the least and the greatest values

5. Mode—the most frequent value of a set of data

6. Median—the value above and below which half the data falls

7. Mean—the simple average

8. Chance—the probability of an event

9. Survey—to question more than one person in order to collect data

10. Scale—a proportion between two sets of dimensions

11. Coordinates—a set of numbers used to show a location on an x and y grid

12. Vertical Axis—a graphing line that is perpendicular to the horizon

13. Horizontal Axis—a graphing line that is parallel to the horizon

14. Frequency—the number of times that a particular event will occur

15. Probability—the likelihood that something will occur

Chapter One

Surveys and Sample Populations

11

Taking a Survey

When you like or appreciate something or someone, you may think that everyone else feels the same way you do. For example, you may like chocolate so much that you cannot imagine that anyone would not like it. The fact is, however, that not all people like chocolate. One way to find out how things are viewed by other people is to take a survey.

You cannot, of course, survey everyone to find an answer to your question; instead you survey a sample group, a portion of the population whose opinion you are seeking. The larger the sample, the more accurate your data will be. A random selection is the most unbiased way to choose a sample group. When you pick people at random, everyone has the same chance of being chosen. There are many ways to choose a random population: draw names from a hat, choose every third person to come along, take only names that begin with certain letters of the alphabet, select a certain number of people from a variety of age groups, etc.

A census is different from a sample as it polls all participants. Although it is more accurate, it is very difficult to administer, so it is seldom used. As a result, people largely rely on the data gathered from sample groups to project how large groups will respond.

It is important that the data collected in a survey is presented to others in a meaningful way. Data can serve as a basis for projecting trends, determining weather patterns, projecting health-related concerns within families, or solving simple business problems. The data from surveys can help to answer important questions.

Think of three questions that you could ask an unbiased sample in order to gather important data concerning your school and the way it operates. Write them here:

1. _____
   _____

2. _____
   _____

3. _____
   _____

Predict the results for each question before you conduct the survey.

Decide how you will determine the population of your random sample. Describe the method you will use in the space below.

You are now ready to take your survey. Create a form that will allow you to represent the choices made by your sample population. In order to simplify the process, you may wish to preselect the choices that are available to those you survey. For example, if your question involves the amount of TV viewing time in a typical week, you may want to have such categories as "About 2 hours," "3–7 Hours," "10–15 Hours," "16–24 Hours," and "25 or More Hours."

Attach your survey form to the back of this page.

Pet Probability

Conduct a survey of at least twenty people in your city asking if they would like to see a zoo established in your area (if there is already a zoo, ask about an aquarium, a petting zoo, or an observatory). Ask about people's interest in animals (or stars), how many times they would visit the new attraction, and if they would support using public funds to help pay for it. Using the information gathered in your survey, write a letter to the city council explaining why you think a zoo (or similar attraction) should or should not be established in your area.

Dear Council Members,

_____

_____

_____

_____

_____

_____

_____

_____

_____

_____

_____

Respectfully,

_____

14

Buggy Business

Working in teams of three or four, collect a sample of data from which you can project a trend.

Scientists want to know about the different insect populations found around schools throughout the country. They have asked your school to send in the most reliable information possible about the insects found in the grassy area closest to the school building. Since it would be impossible to conduct a census to gather this information, you will take a sample and estimate the population of insects for the entire parcel.

Write a paragraph about the way you will solve this problem.

15

Math in the Real World of Business and Living

How Many Drops Make a Drink?

Fill one-third of a small paper cup with water. In a team of three, decide how to most accurately predict the number of drops of water in the glass.

Write your suggestions here:

Test each idea with a dropper to decide which method is the best to use. Describe your results below.

16

Math in the Real World of Business and Living

Chapter Two

Probability

And, Then Again, Maybe Not

When we establish the probability of something happening, we are also establishing the probability that it will not happen. The probability that something will happen plus the probability that it will not happen is always equal to 1 (or 100%). Complete the following:

	Probability that it *will* happen	Probability that it *won't* happen
1.	3 out of 4 times	_____
2.	$^6/_{12}$	_____
3.	_____	.3
4.	1	_____
5.	_____	.58
6.	$^7/_{15}$	_____
7.	_____	$^9/_{22}$
8.	_____	12%
9.	6 out of 11 times	_____
10.	89%	_____
11.	_____	.11
12.	_____	42%

Math in the Real World of Business and Living

The Roll of the Dice

To figure out the probability that a specific number will come up when you roll dice, remember that the probability something will happen plus the probability it will not happen is equal to one. If you roll one die, six things can happen. You can roll a 1, 2, 3, 4, 5, or 6. To find the probability of rolling a 6, figure:

1. How many ways can a six occur? (1)

2. How many different numbers can you roll? (6).

Therefore, the probability of getting a six is ⅙.

Find the following probabilities for one die:

1. What is the probability that you will roll a 5?

2. What is the probability that you will roll a 3 or 1?

3. What is the probability that you will roll a 6, 5, or 2?

4. What is the probability that you will roll a number smaller than 2?

5. What is the probability that you will roll a number larger than 5?

6. What is the probability that you will roll a number larger than 3?

7. With two dice, what is the probability that you will roll a number larger than 10?

8. What is the probability that you will roll a number smaller than 7?

19

Chips Activity

Try your hand at determining the likelihood of something occurring by participating in the "Chips Activity." You, along with five other students, have won a vacation cruise for four with all expenses paid. The Cruise's Prize Committee has called six winners in to claim their cruise prizes.

They have explained to you that the person to draw the most brown chips from the official prize bag will take a cruise to the Hawaiian Islands; the person to draw the most tan chips from the bag will take a cruise to the South Pacific; the person to draw the most yellow chips from the bag will take a cruise to the Gulf of Mexico; the person to draw the most orange chips from the bag will win a cruise to Canada; the person to draw the most red chips from the bag will win a cruise to New Orleans; and the person to draw the most green chips from the bag will win a cruise around the Great Lakes.

Within your group, create a bag of colored chips as follows:
- 12 brown
- 10 tan
- 9 yellow
- 8 orange
- 7 red
- 6 green

Ahead of time, discuss the probability of drawing each of the colors. Then, each student in the group should take a turn selecting a chip from the bag. As each chip is selected, it should not be returned. Make a tally mark in the proper column on the probability chart each time a chip is selected.

As the colors are selected, work in groups of three to set up Probability Tables. The table on the next page will serve as your form. Show the probability of selection both as a fraction and as a decimal. Once you have created your table, write three good questions that you could ask on a separate sheet of paper. For example, you might ask, "What are the odds against selecting a green chip first?"

20

Drawing #	Color	Probability of selection
1		
2		
3		
4		
5		
6		

* If the chips are returned to the bag after each draw and each person drew 100 times, how would the results change?

(Hint): Independent and Dependent Events

If two events happen separately from one another and event A does not influence or depend upon event B, and vice versa, they are independent events.

Example:
1. Three blue chips and one white chip are in Bag A.
2. Two blue chips and two white chips are in Bag B.
3. If you draw one chip from each bag, what is the probability that both will be blue?

You draw one chip from each bag. The result of the draw from Bag A does not influence the draw from Bag B. These are independent events.

You can find the probability of an independent event such as this by multiplying. The probability that both chips will be blue is

A. $P(B) = \frac{3}{4}$

B. $P(B) = \frac{1}{2} = \frac{2}{4}$

$P(B, B) = \frac{3}{4}$ x $\frac{1}{2}$ = $\frac{3}{8}$
       Bag A   Bag B

21

Math in the Real World of Business and Living

If you have only Bag B and you draw a chip from the bag, and, without replacing it, draw a second chip from the bag, you have created dependent events. The outcome of the first draw affects the outcome of the second draw.

To compute the probability of these dependent events, we would use the formula:

$$P(\underset{\substack{\text{1st} \\ \text{draw}}}{B}, \underset{\substack{\text{2nd} \\ \text{draw}}}{B}) = \underset{\substack{P(B) \\ \text{1st} \\ \text{draw}}}{\tfrac{1}{2}} \times \underset{\substack{P(B) \\ \text{2nd} \\ \text{draw}}}{\tfrac{1}{3}} = \tfrac{1}{6}$$

An experience like the "Chips Activity" helps us to take a look at chances and odds. From our selection of chips we know that there are 10 in 52 chances that a tan chip will be drawn on the first try.

We could also say that the odds against getting a tan chip on the first try are 42 to 10. When you are determining the odds against an event occurring, you set up a ratio of unfavorable events to favorable events. You can determine the odds of any event occurring in this manner.

Sock Selection

Think about the familiar problem about socks in a sock drawer. Suppose you have a sock drawer with twelve black socks and six brown socks. What is the probability that you can go to the drawer on a dark morning and randomly select two black socks on the first try?

Answer to Sock Selection

Answer: $12/18 \times 11/17 = 132/306$

You have a 67% (12 of 18) chance of drawing a black sock on the first draw. If you meet this condition, you have a 65% (11 of 17) chance of drawing a black sock on the second try.

Of course, if you get a brown sock on the first try, there is zero probability that a random match on the first two tries will occur.

Math in the Real World of Business and Living

Tasty Probability

In a group of three, develop a probability table for each of the following situations. Write about your findings.

1. You have a small bag of multicolored chocolate candies. If there are 21 brown, 15 red, 16 yellow, 10 orange, and 7 green candies, what is the probability that you will get a green candy when you draw one from the bag without looking?

2. You have a roll of multicolored mints. If there are two mints of each color and there are six colors, what are your chances that the next mint on the roll will be red?

3. You have a box of chocolate cordials. If all the cordials look identical and there are twenty-five cherry, twenty caramel, and fifteen raspberry, what are the chances that you will choose a cherry cordial?

4. You have a box of multicolored candies. There are 21 brown, 15 red, 16 yellow, 10 orange, and 7 green candies. If you only like the green ones, what are your chances of making a good choice if you reach into the box without looking?

Big Max's Burgers and Brats

You have agreed to help Max, a local fast food restaurant owner, at his new burger restaurant. He wants to create burgers the way the customer wants them. Max believes that the customer is always right. Max has a burger menu that can include one or several special choices for each customer. This is what Max has to offer:

Buns	Toppings	Sauces
whole wheat	lettuce	catsup
rye	tomato	dijon mustard
sourdough	cheese	mayonnaise
white	pickles	barbeque sauce
	mushrooms	hot sauce
	olives	

Max has told you that each customer is allowed to have one bread choice, two toppings, and one sauce for the price of $1.69. However, for an extra charge of $0.15 per item, customers may "have it their way."

Create a tree diagram to show the number of possibilities for different types of burgers Max can create for his customers.

Hint: The basic counting principle can be shown with a tree diagram. For example, if **A** can be done in three ways and **B** can be done in four ways, then the two things can be done together 3 x 4 ways. We could make a tree diagram to show the different combinations.

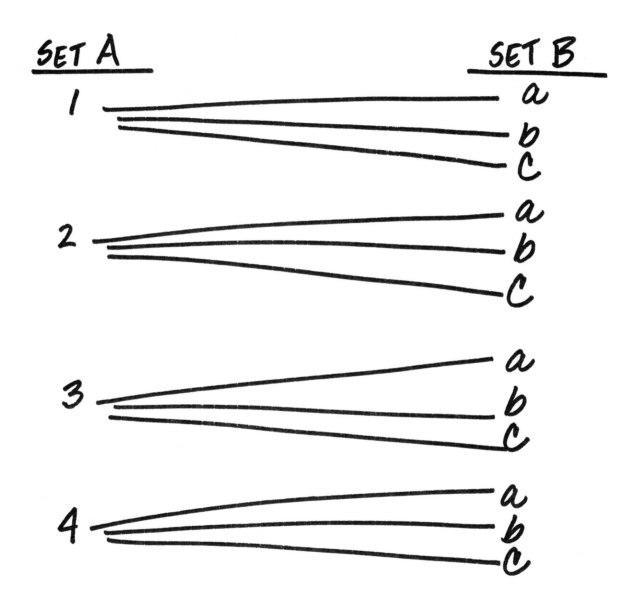

$4 \times 3 = 12$

A combination is a selection of a number of objects from a set of objects without regard to order.

25

The Mysterious Will

A long lost great-aunt died and named you and four other relatives in her will. As she was rather eccentric, she left five mysterious, unmarked envelopes to the five of you. The envelopes have no markings on the outside. The lawyer for the estate has told the family members that each envelope contains either one $50, one $500, one $5,000, one $50,000, and one $500,000.

Instead of giving you your inheritance outright, your great-aunt thought it would be more interesting to make you and your relatives draw for it. Her lawyer has placed the five envelopes in a basket with twenty empty envelopes, and you and your relatives must take turns drawing envelopes until the basket is empty. The stakes are high!

Develop a tree diagram to help you answer the following questions. Assume that your turn to draw will be first.

1. What are the odds against your drawing the envelope containing the $500,000 on the first try?

2. What are your chances of getting all empty envelopes?

3. What are your chances of getting the $50 envelope on the second try?

4. If each empty envelope is placed back in the box after it is drawn, will you have a better or worse chance of choosing an envelope with money? Prove your answer.

26

Math in the Real World of Business and Living

Money Madness

If you flipped a coin, it could land in two different ways. It could land on heads or tails. If you flipped two coins, you could get two heads, two tails, one head and one tail, or one tail and one head.

1. How many combinations can you get if you flipped three different coins?
2. How many combinations can you get if you flipped five different coins?
3. If you tossed five coins, what is the probability that they would land head, head, tail, tail, head?
4. What is the probability that if ten coins are tossed, they will all turn up tails?
5. Can you make a mathematical rule that will describe the number of ways that are possible for any amount of coins to land?
6. How does this rule apply to other real-life situations?

When a group of objects (people or ideas) is arranged in a specific order, the arrangement is referred to as a permutation of the objects. You can find possible permutations by creating a list or chart. For example: Three brothers drive to school together each day. Of course, they all want to drive, or at least ride, in the front seat. To prevent arguments, they created the following chart of permutations:

	1	2	3	4	5	6
Brother A	Drive	Drive	Front	Front	Back	Back
Brother B	Front	Back	Drive	Back	Front	Drive
Brother C	Back	Front	Back	Drive	Drive	Front

You can also find the number of permutations by multiplying.

3	x	2	x	1	=	6
Choices for Driving		Choices for Front Seat		Choice for Back Seat		Total Permutations

A combination of objects is a selection of a few objects from a set of objects, without regard for order. Example: Choose two of the following books to read during the next month.

1. *Number the Stars*   3. *Missing May*
2. *The Haymeadow*   4. *There's a Girl in My Hammerlock*

To find the number of possible combinations:

Permutations of 2 books from 4 books	$\frac{4 \times 3}{2 \times 1}$	=	$\frac{12}{2}$	=	6
Permutations of 2 books from 2 books					

27

Seeing Double?

Popular board games reward players when they roll doubles by allowing them to have an additional turn. Just how difficult is it to get those doubles, anyway?

Record your guess for:

1. The number of times you would
   expect to get doubles
   if you rolled the dice 25 times. _____

2. The number of times you would
   expect to roll the dice
   before you get your first set of doubles.

   _____

Roll two dice 50 times. Keep tally marks for
the number of times you roll and the
number of doubles that you get.

What is the number of doubles in fifty rolls?

Based on this information, how many doubles
would you predict to occur
in 100 rolls?

_____

Roll the dice 100 times. How many doubles
did you actually get?

_____

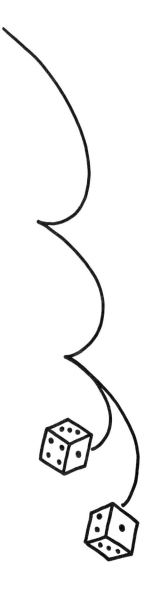

28

Alphabet Soup

Choose a paragraph from a local newspaper. Attach it here.

Predict the number of times you will see each letter of the alphabet in a typical paragraph with 1500 letters. Record your predictions.

a	b	c	d	e	f	g	h	i	j	k	l	m

n	o	p	q	r	s	t	u	v	w	x	y	z

Write the letters of the alphabet on a piece of paper. As you read the paragraph in the newspaper, tally the number of times each letter appears.

Which appears more often, vowels or consonants?

How many total letters are there in the paragraph? What fractional part of the letters are vowels?

What fractional part of the letters are consonants?

Which letter appears most often?

Compare the actual figures to your predictions.

29

Chapter Three

STATISTICS

HOW AVERAGE IS **YOUR** FAMILY?

Statistically Speaking

Conduct a survey, and collect and display data for one of the following questions:

1. What size shoes do the students in your grade wear?

2. How tall are the students in your class?

3. How many people are in the families of the students in your class?

4. Do the students in your class have more brothers or sisters?

5. What is the most common eye color of the students in your class?

6. What is the favorite spectator sport of the students in your class?

7. What is the favorite participation sport of the students in your class? Is it different for boys and girls?

8. What is the favorite subject of the students in your class?

Mean, Median, Mode, and Range

While learning about the mean, median, mode, and range, it will be helpful to have some survey data to work with. Complete the surveys, "All about My Family" (p. 35) and "All about Me" (p. 36). Display your information for other class members to see.

After each survey has been made available to the group, complete the following questions:

1. What is the range in shoe size? _____
   The **range** is the difference between
   the largest number and the smallest
   number on the survey.

2. What is the mean family size? _____
   The **mean** is the sum of all the numbers
   divided by the number of data entries used.
   A synonym for mean is **average**.

3. What is the median height of the family members? _____
   The **median** is the middle number
   when a set of numbers is arranged in order.

4. What is the mode of the ages among the students in your group? _____
   The **mode** is the number that occurs
   most often in a set of numbers.

33

Valuable Information

Create your own questions and answers using the information you gathered from the two surveys. Use mode, median, range, and mean in some way.

Question 1: _____

_____

Answer: _____

_____

Question 2: _____

_____

Answer: _____

_____

Question 3: _____

_____

Answer: _____

_____

Question 4: _____

_____

Answer: _____

_____

34

All about My Family

1. How many people live in your home, including you? _____

   How many males? _____ How many females? _____

2. What color is the house or apartment where your family lives? _____

3. How many TV sets are found in your home? _____

4. How tall is the tallest person in your home?

   _____

5. Do you have a computer

   in your home? _____

6. Do you have a newspaper delivered each week? _____

7. How many glasses of milk does your family drink each week? _____

8. How many cans of soft drinks does your family drink each week? _____

9. What pets does your family own? _____

   _____

10. How many letters do your family members write

    each month? _____

35

All about Me

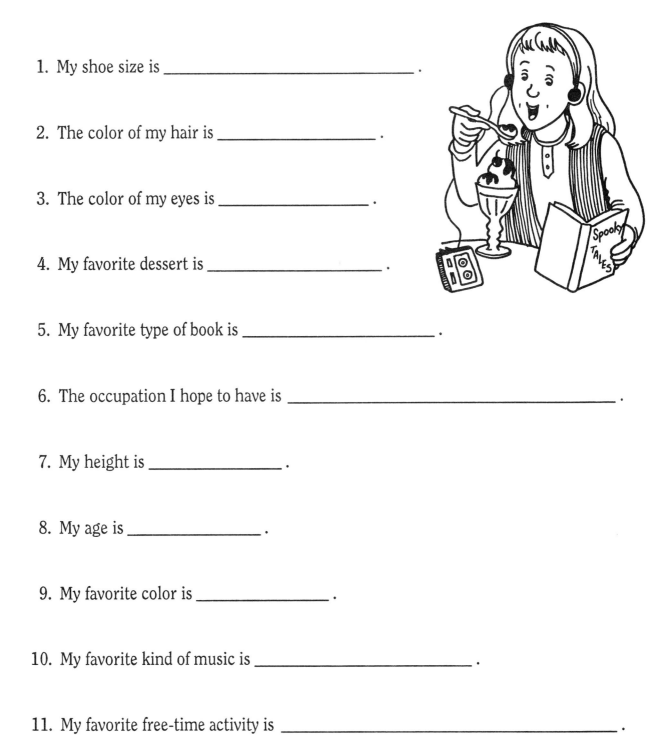

1. My shoe size is _____ .

2. The color of my hair is _____ .

3. The color of my eyes is _____ .

4. My favorite dessert is _____ .

5. My favorite type of book is _____ .

6. The occupation I hope to have is _____ .

7. My height is _____ .

8. My age is _____ .

9. My favorite color is _____ .

10. My favorite kind of music is _____ .

11. My favorite free-time activity is _____ .

Analyzing Data from a Chart

High and Low Normal January Temperatures
(Selected Cities)

City	High	Low
Anchorage, AK	21	8
Asheville, NC	47	25
Atlanta, GA	50	32
Buffalo, NY	30	17
Boston, MA	36	22
Chicago, IL	29	13
Duluth, MN	16	-2
Denver, CO	43	16
Hartford, CT	33	16
Houston, TX	61	40
Jackson, MS	56	33
Little Rock, AR	49	29
Miami, FL	75	59
Minneapolis, MN	21	3
Omaha, NE	31	11
Pittsburgh, PA	34	19
Reno, NV	45	21
San Diego, CA	66	49
Salt Lake City, UT	36	19
Washington, DC	42	27

We can analyze a collection of data and make educated predictions. Analyze the temperature data presented to answer the following questions.

37

1. Which city will likely have the lowest January temperatures this year?

   _____

2. Which city will probably never experience temperatures below freezing?

   _____

3. Compare the temperatures in Anchorage to those in Duluth. Are you surprised? Do you think Anchorage will be slightly warmer again next year? Why or why not?

   _____

   _____

   _____

4. Which city has the greatest range of normal temperatures?

   _____

5. Which two cities have the smallest range of normal temperatures?

   _____

6. In July, the normal high temperature in Chicago is 84 degrees and the low is 63 degrees. If you worked for an advertising agency trying to attract new residents to the Chicago area, what would you write about the weather?

   _____

   _____

7. If you wanted to become a citrus farmer, near which city would you plan to locate? Why?

   _____

   _____

In the Median

There are some interesting pieces of information you can gather at your school that will be helpful in making predictions concerning things to come. Try your hand at one or more of the following.

1. Check with your nurse to see how many students come to his or her office each day for one week. Find the average number to visit during the week. Predict the number of students he or she will see in the following week. Check with him or her at the end of the second week to see how accurate your prediction was. (If possible, collect data for a month.) How will this information be helpful to the people at your school?

2. Check with the librarian to see how many books are checked out of the library each day for one week. What is the median number? Predict the median number to be checked out the following week. How accurate were you? How many books are overdue in a month's time? What can you predict from this?

3. Record the number of students absent from your classroom each day for one week. What can you predict about the following week? (How accurate were you?)

39

Take Your Chances!

Wad up several used sheets of paper or old newspaper. Place a wastebasket about eight feet from you. With a partner, take turns tossing the paper into the basket. Allow each partner to try ten tosses. Record the number of times each partner makes a basket.

	Partner 1	Partner 2
Missed Basket	_____	_____
In the Basket	_____	_____

Calculate the average number of baskets for each person.

Average:	_____	_____

Predict the results of a second set of ten throws. Record your predictions. Then, record the actual results. How valid were your predictions?

Show the average number of successful baskets for each partner as a fraction.

Partner 1	Partner 2
_____	_____

40

Math in the Real World of Business and Living

Newspaper News

Choose a paragraph of information from a local newspaper. Attach it here:

Predict the median length of the words
in the paragraph (number of letters per word). _____

Determine the actual median and record it here. _____

What is the range of word length? _____

What is the mode of the word lengths for this paragraph? _____

What is the mean of the word lengths for this paragraph? _____

41

Plane and Simple Facts

Create a plane using a straw, cardboard, string, and a balloon. Assemble the straw plane as shown below. Stretch the string in between two chairs. Blow up the balloon. Predict how far the straw plane will travel while the air is being released from the balloon. Record the distance in inches.

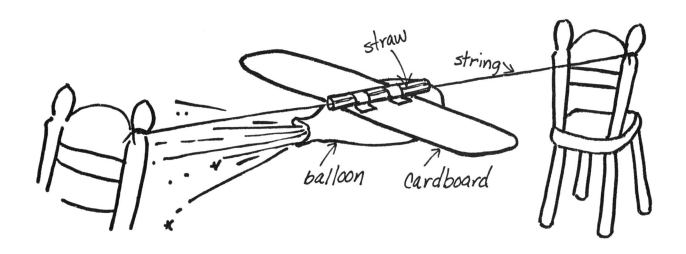

Prediction _____

First try _____

Second try _____

Median distance of all classroom planes _____

Range of all classroom planes _____

Mean of all classroom planes _____

42

The Millionaire's Club

Becoming a millionaire is not a matter of chance. Those who earn a large amount of money through their own hard work rely on statistics to help them make responsible choices. For example, thousands of new restaurants begin business each year in the United States. Within five years, however, only one in five of those new restaurants will still be in operation. That is a survival rate of only 20%. What allows one business to succeed where another fails?

What kind of business do you think would be successful in your community? Design a survey to help you determine if it would be a good business choice. Describe your business idea here. Share your survey results.

_____

_____

_____

_____

_____

_____

_____

_____

_____

_____

_____

_____

_____

Frequency Tables

A frequency table organizes data so that it can be tallied to show how often an event will occur or how many separate occurrences are possible. Complete the frequency table for the data given below.

You work in a shop that sells sports clothes such as sweatpants and T-shirts. One of your foremost clothing manufacturers has come up with a new set of workout clothing with shirts and pants that you can mix and match. Your manager has asked you to figure out how many possible outfit combinations you can create.

You know that if you have two colors of shirts and two colors of pants, you can make four separate combinations: white shirt and white pants, white shirt and red pants, red shirt and red pants, and red shirt and white pants.

Set up a chart like the one here to show the number of different combinations that will be possible with three shirt and pant colors, four shirt and pant colors, five shirt and pant colors, six shirt and pant colors, and seven shirt and pant colors.

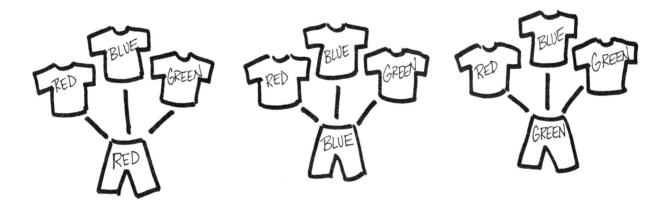

Do you see any type of pattern occurring?

Math in the Real World of Business and Living

Establish a frequency table for the following problem:

You will need one empty paper cup for the experiment. Drop the cup from chest height on 20 different occasions. Record the number of times it lands on its top, bottom, and side.

From the information in the frequency table, what kind of predictions can you make?

Design an original problem that would be easier to work if you constructed a frequency table. Write out the problem, and then construct the frequency table.

45

Chapter Four

Graphing

THE HUMAN HEIGHT GRAPH

Graphing Results

Once data gathering has taken place, results can be presented in a variety of ways. One way to present this information is pictorially through charts or graphs. There are a variety of ways to graph results.

A bar graph is one of the easiest types of graphs to create and use. Quantities are represented by bars. For example, the bar graph below shows the amount of snow that fell each day during one January in the city of Minneapolis, Minnesota.

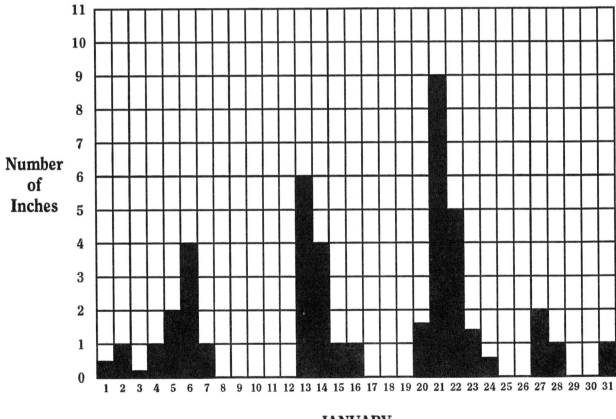

JANUARY

Using information gathered in one of your surveys, create a bar graph to share the results.

Use graph paper so that you can be neat and accurate. Color code your graph and label it clearly.

The Weatherman's Graph

Using the weather report from the newspaper for the last thirty days, construct a bar graph of the highest temperature for each day.

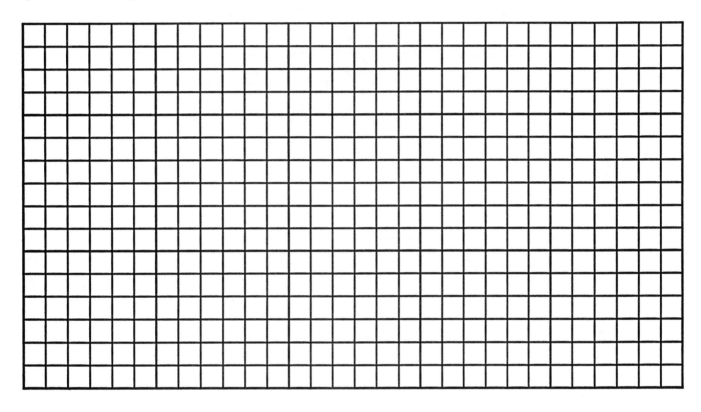

DEGREES

DAY

List two ways that this type of information could be of value to meteorologists.

49

Math in the Real World of Business and Living

The Double Bar Graph

In a double bar graph, parallel bars compare two types of data. For example:

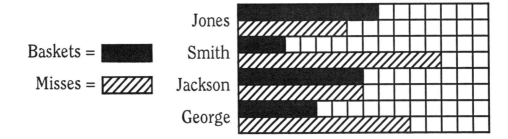

In the "All about My Family" survey, you gathered information concerning how many males and how many females lived in each student's home. Use this information to create a double bar graph in the space below.

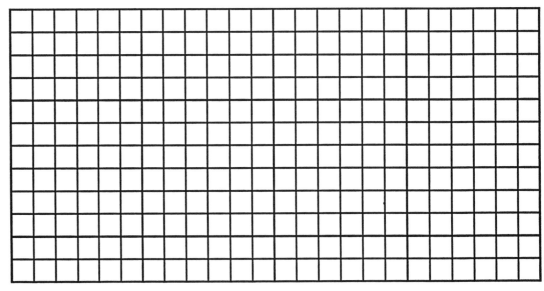

50

Population Boom!?

Create a double bar graph that compares the population for the following ten U.S. states for the years 1980 and 1990.

	1980	1990
Alabama	3,894,025	4,040,587
California	23,667,764	29,760,021
Florida	9,746,961	12,937,926
Kansas	3,660,324	3,685,296
Massachusetts	5,737,093	6,016,425
Nevada	800,508	1,201,833
Rhode Island	947,154	1,003,464
South Dakota	690,768	696,004
Virginia	5,346,797	6,187,358
Wyoming	469,557	453,588

Write a paragraph of information to describe your findings.

_____

_____

_____

_____

_____

_____

_____

_____

_____

The Battle of the Sexes

Using the information gathered in the "All about Me" surveys, create a double bar graph showing the differences between males and females with regard to four key areas.

Write a paragraph of information describing the data that you collected.

_____

_____

_____

_____

_____

Do you think it is more effective to give your information in words or in pictures? Why?

_____

_____

_____

_____

Math in the Real World of Business and Living

Line Graphs

In line graphs, a data line plots through the points of the graph. This type of graph is particularly useful when showing a trend.

Study the line graph below. Discuss the information you can gather from it.

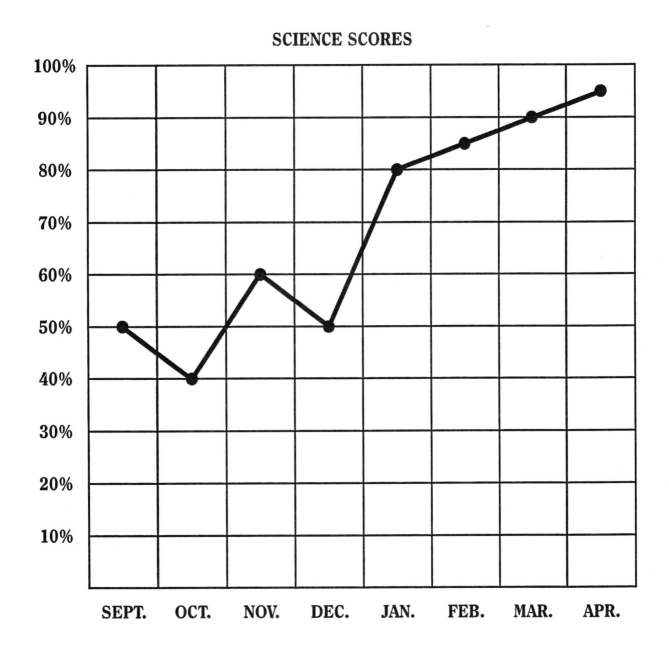

SCIENCE SCORES

Growing Like a Weed

Collect the following data for your growth line graph. You will need to work with several teachers to fill out your data sheet.

How tall is an "average" boy and an "average" girl at each grade level?

Girls   **Boys**

Grade _____   _____   _____

Grade _____   _____   _____

Grade _____   _____   _____

Grade _____   _____   _____

Grade _____   _____   _____

Grade _____   _____   _____

As an alternative, you may wish to talk with your parents and see if you can get your heights for a six- or seven-year span of time. Then compare your results with a person of the opposite sex who has gathered similar information.

Create a line graph showing the results of your data collection. Describe what you discovered. What predictions can you make based on your data sample?

Math in the Real World of Business and Living

Circle Graphs

Circle graphs are used to show how a whole item is divided into parts. The information found on a circle graph is usually presented in fraction, decimal, or percent form.

The following circle graph shows how one family spends their monthly income after taxes. Discuss the information presented on the graph.

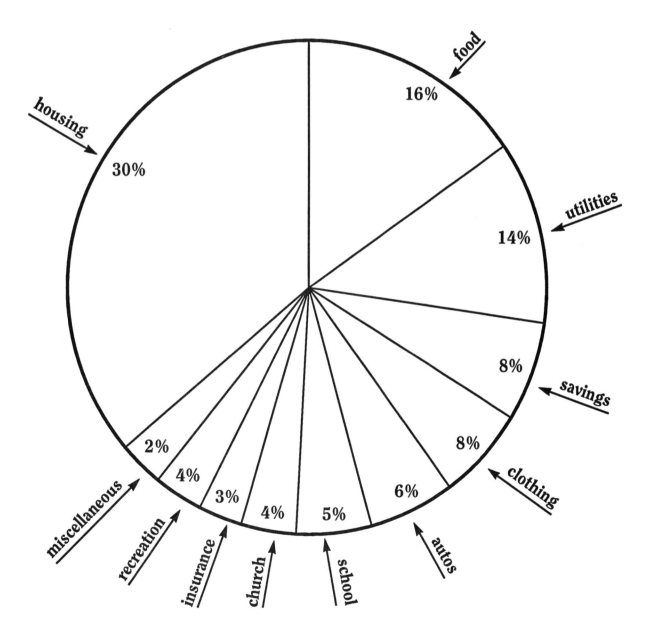

Spending Wisely

Suppose that you earn about $55 per month. You have no consistent monthly expenses but would like to buy a stereo system that will cost about $500. How will you divide your earnings each month? Show this through a circle graph. You will need some money each month for entertainment, snacks, clothes, and savings.

How long will it take to earn the money for your stereo using the spending system you have outlined in your circle graph?

Choosing an Appropriate Graph

Research one of the following questions. Create an appropriate bar, double bar, line, or circle graph to display your findings.

1. Birthday twins are people that share the same birthday. Find out how many birthday twins are in your grade. Graph your findings.

2. How does your heart rate compare to that of your classmates? At rest, determine the pulse rate of at least twenty-five people. How does yours compare? Create a graph to show your results.

3. Create a graph to show the number of male teachers compared to female teachers for each subject matter or grade taught at your school.

4. Find out how often students in each grade eat breakfast each week. Display your findings in graph form.

57

Using Graph Variety

You may use different types of graphs to convey the same information. Graph the information from one of the following charts in two different ways.

When matching graph type to data, consider the following:

1. A line graph depicts change over time.

2. A circle graph shows the relation of parts to the whole and parts to each other.

3. A bar graph is used to compare countable data.

WORLD POPULATION IN MILLIONS—1990
        Africa 661
        Asia 3,116
        Europe 501
        South America 447
        North America 278
        Oceana 27
        (former) USSR 291

SKYSCRAPERS (750 ft. and higher) in 1995
        Chicago 11
        Atlanta 4
        New York 18
        Minneapolis 3

58

Thumbs Up!

Survey your classmates to discover their favorite entertainments. Then create your Thumbs Up Graph to share the data you gathered.

	My Favorite	**My Least Favorite**
1. book	_____	_____
2. movie	_____	_____
3. song	_____	_____
4. female singer	_____	_____
5. male singer	_____	_____
6. singing group	_____	_____
7. TV show	_____	_____
8. snack	_____	_____
9. soft drink	_____	_____
10. pet	_____	_____

59

Home-Sweet-Home Data

Research and graph results for one or more of the following.

1. Find out how much paper your classroom throws away in a week. Compare this amount to that of other classrooms.

2. What is the cheapest way to buy soft drinks—by the six pack, the twenty-four pack, two-liter bottles, or three-liter bottles?

3. How much electricity does your family use each day of the week? Which day do you use the most? Can you find a way to determine which appliance uses the most electricity?

4. Find out how many people carpool in your school. What kinds of savings does this promote?

5. Which takes less water—a shower or a bath? How much water can you save over a year's time by using the least wasteful method of bathing?

6. If your family recycles all of their glass, how much energy will you save?
   Note: *50 Simple Things Kids Can Do to Save the Earth* by The Earthworks Company (Universal Press, 1990) will help you find the information you need.

7. Is it more of an energy saver to recycle glass, newspaper, or aluminum?

8. How many commercials are shown in a typical half hour of television? If all of the commercials were removed, how much more time would the actresses and actors need to perform?

9. If you watch every televised football game in a single year, how many hours of TV will you watch? How does this compare to basketball and football?

10. How much ice cream does a typical four-person family consume in one year? How does this compare to their consumption of frozen yogurt?

11. What is the weight of the junk mail you receive in one day, one week, and one year at your home?

12. How much money does your family spend for utilities in one month? In one year?

Chapter
Five

Data Analysis

Data Analysis

While gathering data and constructing graphs are important functions, they are meaningless if we do not know what the data really means. To use the data constructively, we must be able to analyze it.

Four steps in data analysis:
1. Forming a key problem or question
2. Collecting and organizing data
3. Analyzing and interpreting data
4. Summarizing and reporting your findings

Key Problems or Questions:
Data should be collected in response to solving a significant problem or answering a worthwhile question. The graph then serves the purpose of providing needed information. When you are making a presentation, only graphs that focus on a solution to the problem at hand should be part of the process.

Collecting and Organizing Data:
When you are analyzing data, you need to carefully decide what information is needed to answer the question at hand and how it will be collected. Primary sources of data should be your own surveys and experiments, and secondary sources should be published works such as newspapers, magazines, and reference materials. The Internet is also a wonderful source of current information in a virtually unlimited number of fields.

Analyzing and Interpreting Data:
Computer spreadsheets really come in handy here. You can use a computer to tally data and graph results.
If you are able to graph your results on the computer, examine the data in a variety of graphed forms and contrast the various aspects of the data.
It is important to remember that certain types of graphs better represent different types of data.

Summarizing and Reporting Findings:
It is important to reflect upon and describe your findings. Evaluate and support your conclusions using the data gathered.

Math in the Real World of Business and Living

Data Analysis Sheet

Problem:

_____

_____

_____

_____

_____

Collection of Data:

_____

_____

_____

_____

_____

Data Analysis Sheet, Cont.

Data Analysis:

_____

_____

_____

_____

_____

_____

Summary, Comparison, and Extension of Data:

_____

_____

_____

_____

_____

_____

Real-World Data Analysis
The Restaurant

You have an opportunity to open a new restaurant in your town. You will need to know the types of food that would be the most popular at your new business. Conduct your surveys and analyze the data by following the steps below.

1. Create a survey of the favorite types of food eaten by your friends. Take an unbiased survey to determine the most popular items on your list. Be sure to include main course items, desserts, and beverages.

2. Construct appropriate graphs of the information you have gathered.

3. Discuss the contents of your graphs with your classmates. Do they feel that the contents of the graphs are accurate?

4. Determine the kinds of data that your current graphs do not show. What other information will you need before you can continue on with your business venture?

5. Extend your findings. What should you do next?

65

Math in the Real World of Business and Living

Real-World Data Analysis
The Game Show

Even the busiest of people spend some time watching television. One popular TV format for the past twenty-five years has been the game show. You are in a position to create a new one-half hour game show for prime-time television. Use your survey and data-gathering expertise to find out what type of show will be popular with the general public. Follow the steps outlined here:

1. How will you collect the data that you need to move ahead with your game show design? Would it be helpful to know which game shows are most often watched by a sample of the population? Would information about video game preferences or computer game preferences be helpful? What would be the best broadcast time? Create your surveys based on these and other important questions.

2. Decide how you will collect comparable and reliable data.

3. Tally the data you have gathered and create your graphs.

66

4. From your graphs, determine:
   a. The necessary ingredients needed to create a winning game show
   b. The personnel needed to create a winning game show
   c. Appropriate time slot
   d. Type and amount of advertising
   e. Age of audience watching TV at your time slot
   f. What data is missing

5. Extend your information. Find out if other types of viewing would be preferred by the general public. For example, would they rather see more news broadcasts, cartoon shows, soap operas, or mini-series?

6. Extra Credit: Create an opening show for the game show design that you finally establish. Include, but do not limit yourself to:
   a. The name of the show
   b. The stars of the show
   c. The rules of the game
   d. Prizes awarded
   e. Sponsors

67

Real-World Data Analysis
The Car Dealer

You will be setting up a new car dealership in the area. However, you have not yet decided which particular brand or brands of vehicles you will buy. You have to decide on models, makes, and colors to display on your lot and in your showroom. Use your data-gathering techniques to help you determine the things you will need.

1. Gather data in a variety of ways. Survey friends to determine the make, model, and color of their families' cars. Go to the parking lot and collect data concerning the types of vehicles found there.

2. Create hand-drawn or computer-generated graphs of the information you have collected.

3. Set up an inventory for the new automobile dealership. Support the choices you have made.

4. Have a friend or small group critique the choices you have made.

68

Chapter Six

Real-World Applications

"Think Positive!" News

In newspapers and magazines around the country we read depressing statistics each day regarding local and world problems. You are about to change that! On your own, or as a group, you are going to collect positive research that will lead you to the creation of the "Think Positive!" newspaper. Each individual or team of students will contribute one area of research to the paper.

Create an aesthetically appealing newspaper page after carefully researching for the needed information. As you complete your research, carefully create graphs that will depict your findings as clearly as possible. Remember these rules about graphs:

1. A line graph depicts change over time.

2. A circle graph shows the relation of parts to the whole and parts to each other.

3. Bar graphs are used to compare countable data.

Each graph should be clearly labeled and titled. Remember to clearly define the scale you are using. Samples used must be unbiased.

Positive Pollution Prevention

It is estimated that every time we recycle an aluminum can we save enough energy to power a television for three hours. Research to find out the number of people in your school who recycle regularly. Find out about:

1. Types of materials recycled

2. Energy saved by each material recycled

3. Number of people recycling each material

4. Types of materials that we need to recycle in the future

5. Information regarding levels of pollution today and 10 years ago

6. Companies that we should support due to their energy-saving attempts

7. Energy consumption comparisons around the world

8. Ways that young children can help

9. The latest recycling technology

10. Ways to promote more recycling

71

Math in the Real World of Business and Living

To Your Good Health

People are exercising more today than they were a decade ago as they strive to be healthier. What is some of the good news regarding our health in the United States? Research to find out about:

1. Which diseases have been completely eradicated in the United States?

2. How do deaths from heart disease, cancer, and accidents compare for this decade and the last?

3. Are there any positive statistics to report regarding drug and alcohol abuse?

4. What is happening with infant mortality?

5. How has life expectancy changed in the last 25 years?

6. Interview an older generation to compare the quality of life from one generation to the next.

7. What positive health statistics can you gather at your own school?

8. What are the most encouraging advancements in the health field today?

9. What are students doing to improve their health during their early years? Compare this to the last decade.

Are We Getting Smarter?

Educators and students alike have gotten their fair share of bad press during the last twenty-five years. Scores in key academic areas have been reported to be far below those of students in other countries such as Japan. Create some truthful press by looking at the following areas:

1. How have scores in math and reading changed in the United States during the last ten years?

2. Compare reading scores from students in our country to those of students in other countries where they take comparable tests.

3. How have testing results changed within your school during the last ten years?

4. Survey students regarding their educational objectives.

5. Compare the educational levels of the grandparents of your friends to the parents of your friends.

6. Research to find out how technology has changed the face of education.

7. Is college the answer for everyone?

8. How has subject matter changed during the last decade?

9. How have teaching strategies changed during the last decade?

10. How does time in school compare from country to country?

73

Travel Truths

People have been able to travel farther and faster than ever before during the last ten years. Transportation on the ground and in the air has improved over most of the world. Research to find out about:

1. The latest technology in air and land travel

2. Comparisons of transportation methods around the world

3. Changes in fuel consumption

4. Changes in grades and quality of gasoline

5. Automobile safety

6. Positive automobile design changes

7. Most preferred type of car among families in your school

8. Preferred method of getting to school—walking, biking, riding the bus, traveling by car

9. Average numbers of cars owned per family—changes in last decade

10. Changes in number and type of other motorized vehicles owned by families in your school (snowmobiles, watercraft, etc.)

74

Money, Money, Money

The average American family lives in luxury compared to many people around the world. Just how has our financial picture changed in the last ten to twenty-five years? Research to find out this information:

1. What is the average per capita income in ten countries across the world?

2. How does the buying power of the American dollar compare to ten other currencies?

3. How many students in your class get an allowance?

4. What has happened to the stock market in the last decade?

5. How have wages changed in the U.S. in the last decade?

6. How has inflation compared to economic improvement during the past decade?

7. Compare today's product prices to those of a decade ago.

8. What are some financial advantages that students may have over their parents?

9. How has technology affected our economy over the world?

10. What has happened to the price of technological advances over the last decade?

Crime

The rise in many types of crime is of great concern to everyone. However, there are positive things happening too. Research to find those stories that show how people are working to improve the crime rate within their own communities. Gather information that reflects:

1. Community progress in fighting crime

2. Legislation that is making a difference

3. Prevention programs that are working

4. Early intervention in juvenile crime

5. Rates in crimes such as robbery, assault, car theft, and murder over the last decade

6. Comparing crime rates in the U.S. to crime rates in other countries

7. Changes in the criminal justice system

8. Criminals who have been successfully rehabilitated

9. Reasons for crime and the changes in those reasons during the last decade

10. Ideas for improving the crime rates

76

Math in the Real World of Business and Living

Eating Smart

Today, many people's health problems stem from their poor diets. People consume a large quantity of both sugar and fat. Find out if eating habits have been changing over the last decade and how these changes are affecting people's health.

Consider such things as:

1. The impact of product labels

2. Changes in fat content of a variety of products such as milk, sour cream, etc.

3. Life expectancy around the world—impact of diet on statistics

4. Cost comparisons of more healthy foods and their higher-in-fat counterparts

5. Changes in snack foods over the past decade

6. Soft drink consumption

7. Favorite healthy foods of students in your school

8. Favorite unhealthy foods of students in your school

9. Changes in diet among teachers at school

10. Changes in cafeteria menus over the last decade

11. Number of times an average family eats out in a week

77

In-Depth Study

Everyone is curious about something. Write down five questions that you wonder about.

1. _____

   _____

2. _____

   _____

3. _____

   _____

4. _____

   _____

5. _____

   _____

Choose the question that is of most interest to you. Create a web of key words concerning your question.

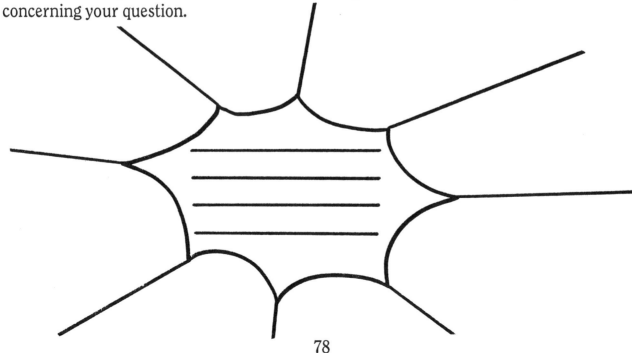

78

Math in the Real World of Business and Living

Focus on one key area of your question. For example, your initial question might have been, "How important is popcorn as a snack food in the United States and Canada?"

You might focus your question to deal with the expansion of popcorn production over a several year span of time.

After conducting your research, you would put together a variety of graphs such as the ones that follow.

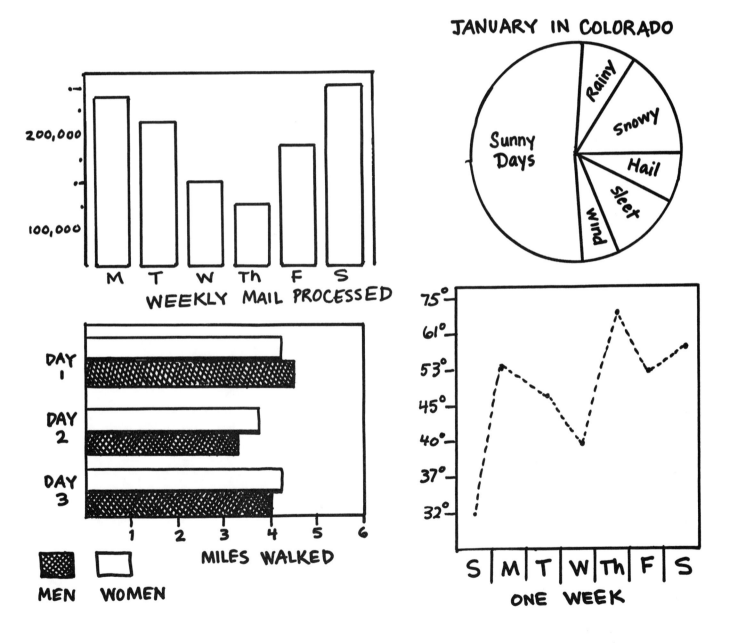

In-Depth Study Graphing

Key Question: _____

_____

_____

Graphs of important information (create two or more):

Creating Stories from Graphs

You will be given several graphs of information. Some of them will be fictional, and some of them will be factual. Study each of the graphs carefully.

Choose a graph from the following pages that you feel is particularly interesting. Look over the information contained in the graph and begin taking notes about the facts that you can discern from the graph.

You are going to use these facts to write a creative short story or poem. It must be evident from the contents of the story or poem that you are very familiar with the information provided by the graph and that you have analyzed it accurately.

Your story or poem should follow the conventions of good literature. Be sure to create a title for your work.

Ask a friend to read your literary creation once you have completed it. Then ask them to create a graph of the important information that the story provides. Tell them which graph form you want them to use.

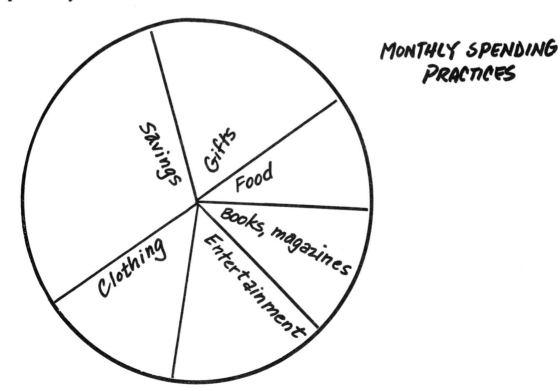

81

MONEY EARNED

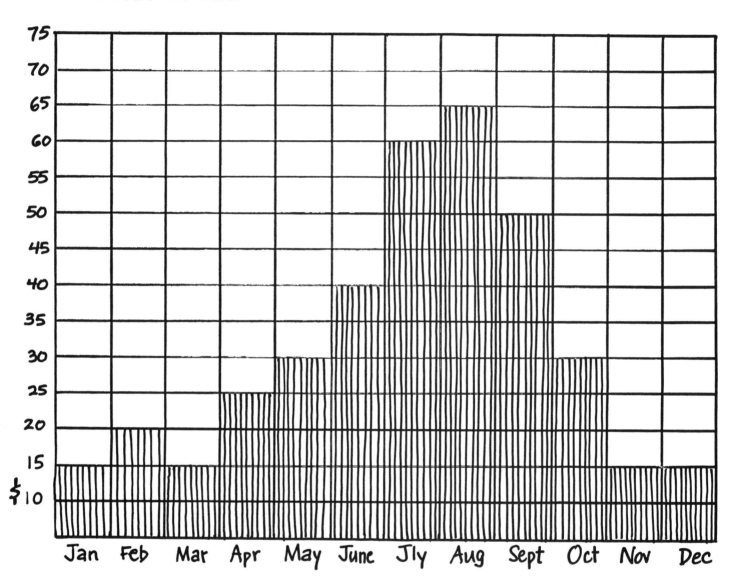

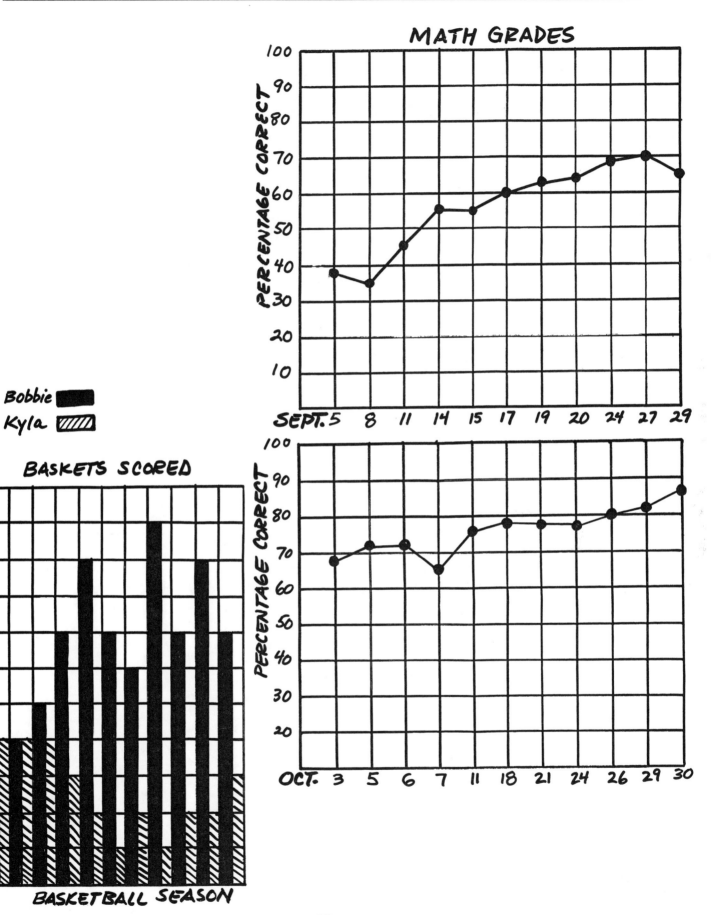

MATH GRADES

Bobbie ▮
Kyla ▨

BASKETS SCORED

BASKETBALL SEASON

83

Creating a Graph from a Story

We often think of graphs as providing us with numerical data and nothing more. However, we know that graphs can show trends, predict future happenings, provide contrasts between differing groups, show increases and declines, show changes in composition, and show a variety of other important things.

Can we show a story line through a series of graphs? Follow the steps outlined here to do just that.

1. Choose a favorite short story. It can be any story that you have read or have had read to you during your lifetime.

2. Clearly delineate the beginning, the middle, and the end of the story. Write down important facts about each of these story parts.

3. Decide on an appropriate type of graph that you could use to show each of these story sections. Remember to label your graphs clearly and show a scale when needed.

4. At the top of your page show the name of the story and the author.

5. When you have completed your three graphs, share them with a friend. Ask your friend to retell the story to you based on the information found in your graphs.

This is the saddest story I've ever read...

84

Spinner Game Number One

Using the guideline for making a spinner (see pages 89 and 90), create a spinner with eight equal parts. Color two of the parts red. Color three of the parts yellow. Color one part blue and two parts green. Two partners will play this game together. First guess which color the spinner will land on, then spin it and record your result on the chart. Taking turns with your partner, record your guesses for twenty-five spins each.

What mathematical formulas can you derive concerning the number of times that each color will come up on the spinner?

_____

_____

_____

Spinner Game Number Two

Spinners can be designed with any number of equal parts. Look at the spinners pictured here. Predict the number of times each letter or color will come up in fifty spins of the spinner.

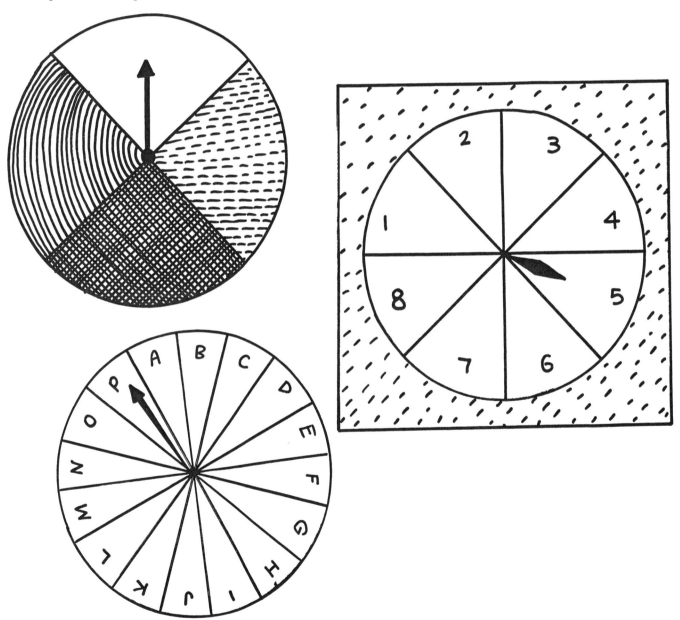

Create one of the spinners and try it out.

Math in the Real World of Business and Living

The Organized Spinner

Create a four-part spinner. Color one section red, one section blue, one section yellow, and one section green.

Can you guess the order in which the colors will be chosen when you spin your spinner four times in a row? For example, one order would be red, red, blue, green.

How many orders are possible? _____

Try twenty sets of four spins and record your results here:

_____   _____   _____   _____

_____   _____   _____   _____

_____   _____   _____   _____

_____   _____   _____   _____

_____   _____   _____   _____

87

We Want Pizza!

At Menlo Park Middle School the students wanted to see pizza on the cafeteria menu more often. The cooks offered pizza four times every month. The Student Council wanted to have more voice in the choices for lunch and went to talk with the cooks. The cooks didn't object to serving pizza, but wanted more variety to their menu. They decided to come up with a democratic solution to the problem.

At the beginning of each day, a student from Menlo Park would meet with the cooks and their huge spinner of menu items. The cooks had created a large wheel with five pie-shaped sections. Each section contained the main course item for five different meals. The student would spin the spinner, thus determining the menu choice for the following day. The sections of the wheel contained hamburger, chicken, pizza, macaroni and cheese, and lasagna.

Based on the information given, predict the number of times students are likely to have pizza in a four-week period.

Create a spinner that would help them improve their odds.

88

Making a Spinner

You will need: cardboard, paper clips, paper punch, scissors, ruler, pencil, and tape.

1. Cut out the cardboard pointer and punch a hole in the center. Tagboard will be fine.

2. Cut a small square of cardboard to serve as a washer and punch a hole in the middle.

3. Cut out a five-inch square of cardboard and divide it into four equal parts. Make light pencil lines to show the divisions. Put a small hole in the center with your paper clip.

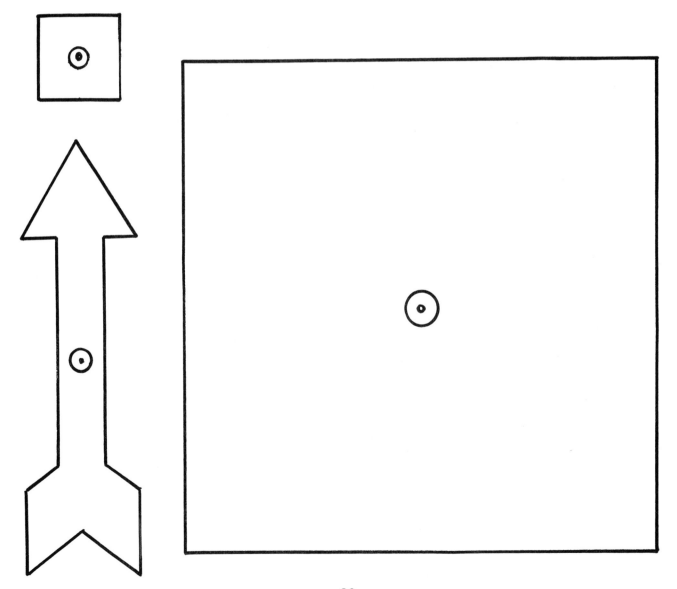

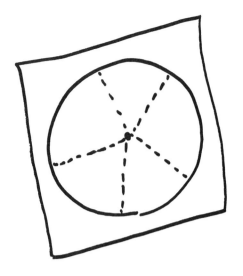

4. Use a compass to make a circle within the square. You may wish to wait to divide the spinner into parts when you know how many parts you will need. Color your spinner and pointer.

5. Bend your paper clip into a 90 degree angle.

6. Tape the loop of the paper clip to the bottom of the square and put the paper clip through the center hole. Add the paper washer and the pointer.

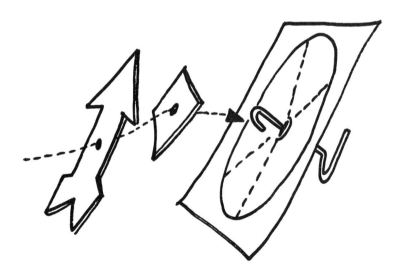

Metric Graph Paper

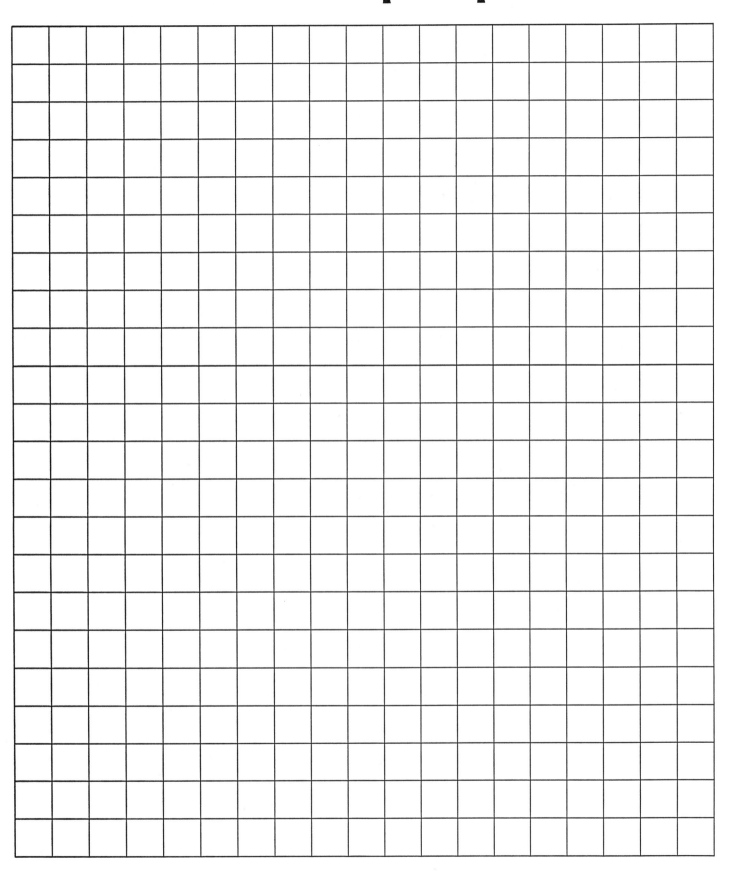

¹⁄₂-Inch Graph Paper

1/4-Inch Graph Paper

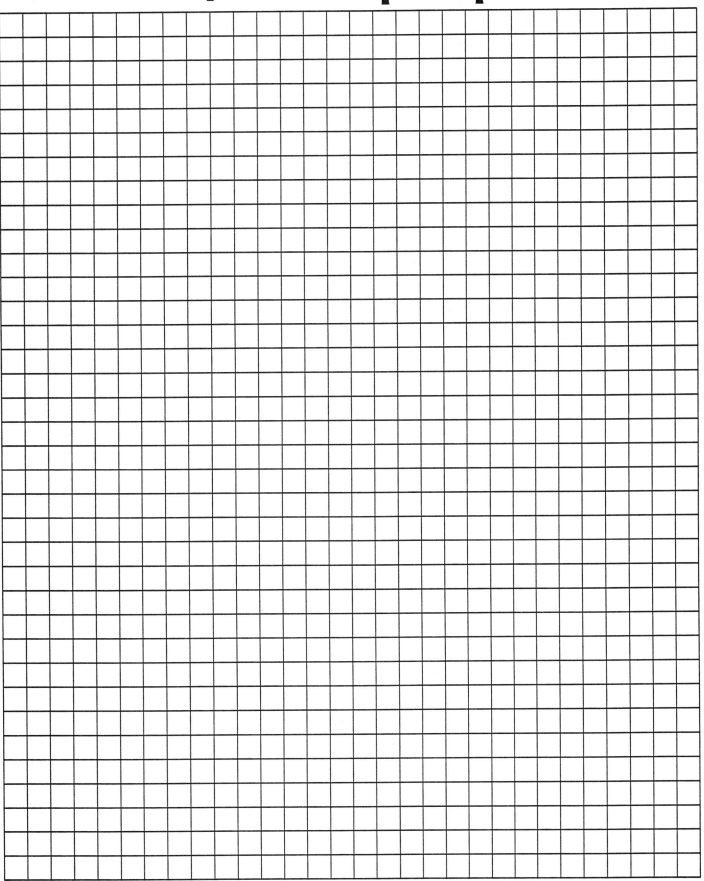

Large Circle Graph

Small Circle Graph

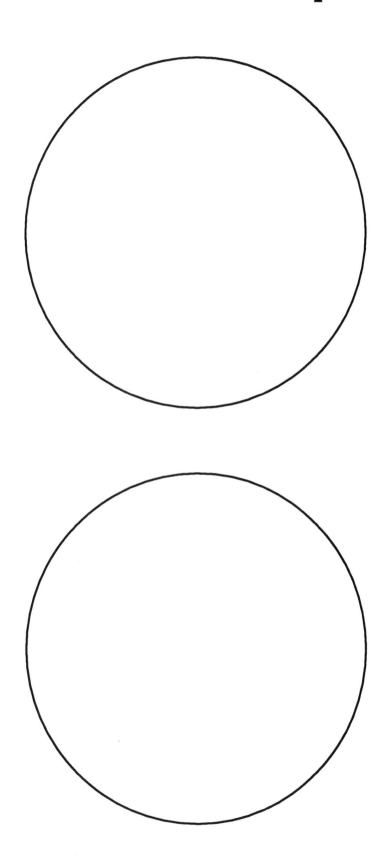